Memento Mori
A Poetic Memoir in Three Parts

poems by

Eileen Porzuczek

Finishing Line Press
Georgetown, Kentucky

Memento Mori
A Poetic Memoir in Three Parts

Copyright © 2025 by Eileen Porzuczek
ISBN 979-8-89990-133-1 First Edition
All rights reserved under International and Pan-American Copyright Conventions. No part of this book may be reproduced in any manner whatsoever without written permission from the publisher, except in the case of brief quotations embodied in critical articles and reviews.

ACKNOWLEDGMENTS

I would like to thank my family and friends for being there for me unconditionally and supporting me throughout everything. Without all of them, I wouldn't be where I am today.

I'd also like to thank Finishing Line Press for publishing *Memento Mori: A Poetic Memoir in Three Parts*, my debut poetry collection, and providing me with a platform to share my story.

Publisher: Leah Huete de Maines
Editor: Christen Kincaid
Cover Art: Maghfur Imam
Author Photo: Samone Malone
Cover Design: Elizabeth Maines McCleavy

Order online: www.finishinglinepress.com
also available on amazon.com

Author inquiries and mail orders:
Finishing Line Press
PO Box 1626
Georgetown, Kentucky 40324
USA

Contents

Part I

self care September	1
a college student's dinner	2
when things collapse death arrives	3
bloody mary	5
incoherent	6
wait what	7
you think you peed	8
good luck, there's something stuck	9
let me take care of you	10
do you even recognize yourself	11
frantic fear	12
pose and wait	13
doctor, doctor give good news	14
painfully numb	15
you're rotting	16
it's happening	17
tears of joy	18
you hate Jell-o	19
aquaphor and pineapple cores	20
a warm welcome back	21
they say they can't tell	22
stop staring	23

Part II

let's make a deal	27
help me fight	28
don't say it's the end of the line	29
parallel universes collide	30

a new normal 32
no communication 33
therapy the flashbacks away 34
many nights on martin st 35
insects crawl to the surface 36
learning to dive your face 37
silicone slumbers 38
be prepared 39
good cop, bad cop 40
there will be no pancakes today 43
rally and finish this 44
muscles don't relax when tension is home 45
thanks, Country Bears© 46
time passes 47
but wait, there's more 49
snakes are alive and well 50
can we settle this 53

Part III

26 months later 57
reflective awakening 58
you are the wolf 59
EMDR 60
the brain waters the aloe plant 61
you've outgrown him 62
embrace you 63
you are 64
let him in and see the flowers bloom 66
memento mori 67

This poetry collection is dedicated to anyone who has ever lived through trauma, been forced to defend their traumas, or had to navigate moving forward with resilience.

Part I

self care september

trapped inside a coffin, yet no panic
there is singing, there is smoking
a moment of carving reflection,
the wooden ceiling now placing
memento mori into the rapper's face…

there is no escape, just him,
him and the coffin ceiling.
remember, remember that
like september you'll fall.

with a deep breath, his tightened fist
lays close against letter's grooves.
then in one calculated movement…
the coffin ceiling has buried him.

you gasp in awe, *is the music video over*?
but before you turn it off, he emerges—
he emerges from the debris and sings,
he sings about how he sees different now.

and in an instant you feel something,
something you cannot quite explain.
this is your new favorite music video,
at least in September of 2018.

a college student's dinner

dinner, dinner, dinner,
what to have for dinner?

hmmmmmmmm

a frozen filet of tilapia
a 99 cent ramen noodles package
and fresh leafy spinach

this will make a fine dinner.

boil the water and see little, tiny bubbles flowing in sync.

the flavor packet mixes itself into the water like blood staining everything in its path.

drop the hard curvy noodles with a hint of Cayenne Pepper
(you like it hot).

now the tilapia is the star, you rub spices along its naked raw body.

spices open nostrils with warmth.

time to fry.

the barren pan now filled with hot frying olive oil, oil that sizzles the fish flesh with no mercy.

back to the ramen, it's draining time.
a stampede of hot steam clouds your face.

sweat in a sauna now.

but wait, don't forget the fresh spinach, it must be wilted.

take the wilted spinach out of the pan—it's damaged now.

clean, clean with the pomegranate dish soap you love.

when things collapse death arrives

Hey K, do you think we could…

BOOM.

there is nothing. absolutely nothing.
no sight, no touch, no taste, no smell,
a limp body half-conscious in view.

the weight weighs heavily and ails,
it pushes down and crushes flesh.
then there is a life-saving palm,
hold on tight to its golden strand.

coming to, but unable to breathe,
you look at K alarmed as if to say,
help me please I cannot breathe….

arms wrapped tightly, he rushes to
do the Heimlich—fearfully thrusting,
pressing on your body. every moment
you feel less—your time is limited now.

memories, loved ones, fill your mind—
but death doesn't wait for reflection.
make peace, say goodbye, it's the…

cough. cough. cough.

blehhhhhhhhhhh

huh huh huh huh

brown insulation, metal, and a piece of ceiling…
wait how could that be?
catch your breath in a fiberglass filled throat,
and confusedly mutter, *what happened K?*

pale faced and eyes wide, K just stares,
terrified of what he sees staring at him.
you can see his mind calculating words,

the ceiling collapsed on you;
i think you should go look in the mirror while i find our phones.

bloody mary

blood.blood.blood.
is that me or bloody mary?

warm thick blood reflects in the mirror, distorting your face—
like red fruit punch aggressively mixed with vodka at a frat party.

bloody mary would've felt elated to see her face covered like yours,
at least according to Lore, it was part of her beauty regime.

but *beautiful* is the farthest thing from what you feel right now—
let alone anywhere near what you see looking back at you.

with a wash cloth in hand, you slowly blot the blood off,
dab by dab, until you see a red snot like clot clinging to your cheek.

gulp.

swallowing burns your throat, but nothing can shake your attention,
gently you pull it off your face, watching it hang in one piece.

the floating blood looms in the air, reminding you of the mortality of life,
until you place it in the sink and watch it wash away within an instance.

if bloody mary were there, perhaps she would've used it as a face mask,
or maybe just eaten it—you're lucky she wasn't there to devour your flesh.

incoherent

body
        dragging.

face
        numb.

K places you in the car.

throat
        slashed.

heart
        racing.

Father John Misty plays from his phone.

mind
        drifting.

voice
        silent.

girl what are people gonna think?

wait what

gripping onto K for dear life,
shuffling into the sliding ER doors,
shaken in your fiberglass clothes and skin,
you approach the check-in counter.

how may i help you?

her question bringing you back to reality.

umm...a ceiling just collapsed on me and i need medical attention, i feel like i am struggling to breathe, my throat is burning, and i can't feel the entire left side of my face—it's just numb.

all eyes behind the desk swiftly stare,
and suddenly you're an art exhibit—
an anomaly they can't help but
feast their eyes on in shock.

page after page, question after question,
you manage to finish their questionnaire—
all the while K's face remains pale and stale,
texting your parents' updates from the waiting chair.

Eileen, we can help you now.

the hospital bed is green and hard with sanitary paper,
you feel it's cold surface against your back in the hospital gown.
once again, they ask you what happened and reply in disbelief,
wait, what happened? you might as well be a broken record.

you think you peed

loaded with prescription painkillers,
they wheel your bed to another room
to scan your face and throat—after all,
you're adamant something is stuck.

with a helping hand, you're situated,
ready for the big scan to take place—
but inside you scream, terrified of
that claustrophobic circular machine.

3...2...1

it's happening, there's no turning back now.

you're in the machine, it has you hostage like
the ceiling that trapped you earlier that night.
just breathe, just breathe, you tell yourself with
eyes closed as warm tingles trickle down your legs.

oh no, did i just pee...i think i peed...

and just like that, the big scan is over,
time for you to get back to your room.
back to the pale faced boyfriend waiting,
waiting to give your parents the next update.

good luck, there's something stuck

in and out. in and out. you strain to breathe.
the albuterol passing through your cut throat—
squeezing past the swollen meatball tissue.
it's on a journey to repair burned lungs with life.

trauma adrenaline the only thing keeping you
both awake and on edge—eyes are bloodshot.
the waiting, the waiting, the waiting, is killer,
and ironically, you just want to lay in your bed.

both doctor and nurse return with more news,
by now they've surely seen the scan's results.
sharing a brief look, the nurse puts away the
breathing treatment machine as the doctor speaks,

so, we can't really tell what's stuck or really say...
but you must see an ENT because something is stuck.

you try to ask questions, you try to get information,
but both doctor and nurse refuse to tell you more.
take your prescription slip, put on your clothes, and
walk out the door...they can't help you anymore.

let me take care of you

K can see the hurt in your eyes,
it's taking all he has not to cry.
walk into the 24-hour drug store—
body sluggish with a shaken core.

the man at the prescription counter stares at
your bandaged face wanting to have a chat.
but, he just takes your doctor slip, no I.D. needed—
your face genuinely just looks that fucked up.

you walk over to sit down in a waiting room chair,
but K tells you that you'll need to eat something.
Garden Salsa Sun Chips and take-home medical gauze,
not a combo you thought you'd need earlier…you pause.

back at your apartment, you remove your fiberglass clothing,
wash your fiberglass skin, and scrub debris out of your hair.
six rounds of body wash, shampoo, and conditioner later,
you're finally clean, ready to sleep. K holds you as you drift away.

do you even recognize yourself?

bright beaming yellow walls,
covered with painted flowers
surround you in the sunshine,
a vivid place of joy and safety.

but you don't wake up here,
you're no longer safe in your
childhood sanctuary. instead,
you're wounded, this is reality.

in the mirror you see yourself,
you see the bandage on your face.
pre-emptively wincing as you
pull it off, but nothing is felt.

is that me…is that my face…?

wait, why is there a hole in my face?

why can i see my insides?

entranced in the horrific sight,
you stand there and stare.
the mucus skin outline so tight,
it's more than your eyes can bare.

leaning in, intent on a closer look,
torn facial tissue and reddened veins
cry for help like a damsel in a book—
crawling away from imminent death lane.

this isn't something you can solve,
not a problem only for an ENT's hands—
oh no, this will take time to resolve—
hopefully your body can withstand.

in your heart you know who you need,
just ask them for help before you bleed.

mom, dad, i need help finding a doctor…something just isn't right.

frantic fear

lup-dup | lup-dup | lup-dup

your heart beats to sounds of your peanut songs' playlist,
humming in the background as you gather your things.

frantically, cascading across the room packing life up—
you will live out of this bag for the next 2-weeks.

waiting, you erratically scrub dishes till hands are raw,
but nothing distracts from the gauze on your torn face.

dad has arrived and you're off—off to the scary unknown,
a place of twisting and turning cloudy uncertainty.

silently, the two of you sit in the car—him driving
and your brain working overtime as you eat wings.

*so, i found a plastic surgeon—who's an ENT—
she can see you today. we are going there now.*

holding back tears and fiery vomit, you think about how
much this will cost and the funds in your bank account.

sensing the thick cement mixture of tension and fear,
filling your eyes, he continues to break silence.

*this is your face, there's no being cheap about it...we
will figure it out, just focus on healing.*

warm salty tears that once puddled in your eyes now fall hard—
an Adam's needle plant would love to collect these.

pose and wait

the sterile office was a well-defined playground
for curated Stepford Wives—a common species.
they sat there eating cookies, drinking champagne,
and scheduling their next Botox or facial operation.

what plastic land is this?

the gauze covering your face didn't really fit in—
you were a sore thumb in a room full of toes.
unwanting for chit chat, you hung your head low,
waiting to be called, waiting for an answer.

the first room was small—not private—
and made for taking before and afters.
removing the gauze to expose your face,
the photographer's eyes grew bigger.

sit on the green stool and pose for me.
i will take photos of your face from every angle.

the rotting crater in your face fully displayed,
tightening with each wisp of air passing by.
not wanting to pose, but complying, you sit
and turned. *can i put the gauze on now?*

tick tock. tick tock. tick tock.

now you wait. you and your dad just wait.
sit in silence, twiddle your thumbs, look at
the doctor's degrees on the wall—just do
whatever you can to pass the waiting time.

neither of you say much, just waiting for someone
to walk in with news. but 45-minutes pass, and
still nothing. stomach churning in pain you feel
cemented in shame, here comes full disassociation.

doctor, doctor give good news

doctor, doctor give good news, lift spirits and heal flesh wounds.

first thing, the ER doctors didn't properly clean your face—
there is still dirt in the wound.

second thing, without seeing your scan i can't say exactly what is stuck.

third thing, regardless, your skin is already decomposing and
you need surgery immediately.

oh doctor, doctor this isn't good news…head pounding and eyes glazing, this isn't so easy to swallow through the swollen fiberglass tunnel.

oh doctor, doctor give good news, maybe it's not as
bad as it sounds…

we must do a complete facial reconstruction of
your left cheek tomorrow morning.

your entire being begins to shut-down, you are fluorescent office lights being turned off, *click, click, click* at closing time. things continue to happen around the husk of your body but you won't let yourself cry, just go through the motions and get home.

painfully numb

blackened, charred skin festers on your face,
but exudes no pain—just hardened tightness.
thick aquaphor greases and moistens the base,
soothing infested flesh and bone with kindness.

look in the mirror, look in the camera, reflect
and see what you are now destined to be.
what if you didn't stay? no time to deflect.
how you wish for a time rewind for you to flee.

can you feel anything or are you just painfully numb?

share the pain, the fears with K—get some warmth.
let him comfort you with…*you're being overly dramatic,*
but you must like that because you stay thenceforth.
or maybe you worry no one will love you and panic.

you want to feel, to be alive outside of the trauma.
but you are numb, everything is completely numb,
if only you had a Merriweather, Flora, and Fauna.
all you can do is wait and see what it will become.

you're rotting

wake up, do you feel yourself rotting?
things are much worse this morning,
you don't even know they're plotting.
look in the mirror and start mourning.

it's dying, crackling, frying to a crisp—
like tilapia flesh in a non-stick pan.
it's drying, hardening, a dead wisp—
like spinach wilting according to plan.

can you feel the flesh decomposing?
does it make your insides squirmy—
like meat in your stomach exposing
a treacherous, sick, and foul journey.

you're rotting, but can do nothing.
oh yes, fully rotting, that's the thing.

it's happening

good morning sunshine it's happening,
today is the big day you're waiting for.
after all, today is the day you get your
new face constructed—your mask.

wake up, and drug up, you'll need it today.
Hydrocodone and Valium, a candy elixir—
not that you could even feel anything,
the left side of your face is still numb.

shower, get dressed, pick up your scan,
get in the car and head to the doctor.
you can't even balance to walk, *can you?*
no matter, your parents help guide you.

it's posing time again, so remove the gauze.
see the shock in their faces as they realize
just how quickly you're rotting, skin charred
and hard—*will the damage be salvageable?*

lay in the operating room chair, and try to relax.
doctor and nurse are with you now, time for some
Twilight—exactly what you needed to go over the
edge. so, say goodnight, and into the oblivion you go.

tears of joy

it's over, you're awake now and
they did everything in your sleep.
open those groggy eyes and look,
look into the tiny handheld mirror.

that's you, that's your new face—
still healing of course, but still, look.
sit in the wheelchair and journey to
see mom and dad, they're waiting.

you're with them now, they're teary
eyed and crying tears of joy. this new
face must be an improvement from
your injured blackened salmon skin.

we removed insulation, metal, and a piece of ceiling lodged 2-inches deep.

*if your cheekbones weren't strong enough the impact would have
shattered them and made a hole through you face and into your mouth.*

some of your facial nerves were torn, they may heal or may not.

doctor continues with care instructions,
but you're too high to process them.
instead, your parents take detailed notes,
it's time to head home now and rest.

you hate jello

jello, jello, jello, where to begin?

ah, yes, we don't get along—but still
cross paths when you sense sickness.
dad grabs the box off the shelf at the store—
thoughtfully—but you disgust my soul.

the thick gelatin—animal bones, skin, and
cartilage—make vomiting sound delightful.
but the food coloring is what brightens layers
up, what makes everyone want a little taste.

without a filter, you can't hold it in anymore,
i know dad got me Jell-o and i absolutely hate jello.

aquaphor and pineapple cores

aquaphor your greasy new best friend,
pineapple cores your new favorite food.
you never knew you needed them till
now—they are your new face's lifeline.

outside of these, you can't do much…
no eating meat or dairy, no raising your
heart rate—no hands above the head,
you can't even shower and bath yourself.

aquaphor to ensure the healing incision
stays moist and hydrated, no drying or
cracking. it's clear ointment covering
even bandages for good measure.

pineapple cores, the center of a fruit
you never liked—you must eat it now.
it's like a magical potion for your skin,
an all-natural way to heal and glow.

a full week of sitting, only moving from
location to location—with help, of course.
you've grown terribly tired of aquaphor and
soy ice cream blended with pineapple cores.

K visits you and the tension is heightened,
mom and dad never really liked him for you.
maybe because of the time he hit you, or
maybe it was when he stole your debit card.

still, he saved your life and you care for him…
you don't know what it would take to leave.
soon you'll have to leave the safety of home
and head back to school, back to the reality.

a warm welcome back

the time has come for you to return,
but you're frightened to see their eyes.
scared to face the unknown reactions
that await you—*what will they think?*

mom and dad drive you back safely with love.
K is there to greet you with flowers and a kiss.
next stop picking up your sister at her dorm, it's
time for Hot Tofu Pad Thai served with a smile.

settle back into your room and read the card.
roomies tell you what a beautiful person you are,
how they're so happy you survived—you matter.
enjoy the decorations and wear the bracelet.

they say they can't tell

they look at you and say they can't tell,
but you know they're either blind or lying.
forcing a plaster smile you try not to dwell,
you know they love you so they're denying.

it's painful, this fraudulent tango you dance,
both moving in perfect sync—no honesty.
it's hard knowing truth, hearing their stance,
but you really can't tell—promised he.

can you see them staring closely?
does it make you uncomfortable—
like fiberglass sitting in you grossly.
the lies are becoming insufferable.

they say they can't tell, but it's a lie.
the lies they tell your eyes make you die.

stop staring

wandering eyes follow where ever you go,
their cold icy stares pierce into your soul.
tracking and haunting as if to say hello,
judging you like a kid getting a lump of coal.

on and on they stare, not knowing their damage.
they leave you tense, wanting so badly to scream—
but you stay silent, somehow you'll manage.
even with caked makeup you feel a low self-esteem.

never ever did you know the pain of a stare,
how does it make you feel to be the fish in a bowl?
you used to be like them and stare without a care,
but now you know the pain it causes Eileen Nicole.

please stop staring, i am not your attraction,
but no, don't cry and give them the satisfaction.

Part II

let's make a deal

you did nothing wrong, almost died—here's the bill.
no one will accept fault and pay; this will not be easy.
fight with all your might—gather and sharpen tools.
phone a friend, write a letter, mail it off, and wait.

time passes, weeks, a month, maybe even more,
but nothing—has your plea fallen on white noise?
enjoy the little moments you have, watch those
Rankin and Bass Christmas Specials you love.

the phone will ring and dad will answer the call.
it's them, shattering the ominous silence with
pungent words, *hire a lawyer or we don't care.*
not exactly the Merry Christmas you wanted.

help me fight

the steps of the historic military house are preserved,
sitting in a little neighborhood of other fort homes.
it's just you and your dad today, and the weather,
well, the Indiana weather is cold with an icy bite.

the conference room is empty, besides the refreshments.
the two of you sit down with nothing to do but wait—
this is not how you imagined spending the holiday season.
a lawyer walks in, he is tall and in a fine suit…here we go.

you bare the trauma of what happened in under 10-minutes,
he has questions and you have answers—a questionnaire ensues.
the lawyer is silent for a moment…thinking over the information,
determining whether they would take on your unfortunate case.

please help me fight, please i can't let them brush this under the rug.

your plea repeats in your head, a symphony of pain and panic.
lucky for you, they believe in your fight and will take the case.
but no promises on the result, they've never had a case like this,
only facial dog bite cases—this will be new for the both of you.

don't say it's the end of the line

emotions stay bottled up as ulcers,
you've never felt so left to the vultures.
a longing for K lives inside your heart.
but the waves move you further apart.

you need him, but he doesn't care…
crying, the bottles now pouring impair.
but your roommates offer compassion.
they are your angels loving without ration.

K makes a final appearance, not sincere.
i'm done being there for you—are we clear?

you kick him out and it's officially over,
you don't need his unlucky 3-leaf clover.
let the drunken, sad musician go on—
this time you've gotta stay strong.

parallel universes collide

he hurt you,

    he lied,

        you leave.

---

he hurt you,

    he lied,

        you know this, but you stay.
        maybe it's because he thought he loved you,
        or maybe it's because you're too comfortable—
        still, you stay.

            time passes

            you cook him dinner,
            you visit and sit on his bed—
            try your hardest to maintain what's left.
            still, not enough.
            you're practically swallowing your pride
            something needs to wake you.
            a force unknown will do the bidding,

            BOOM.

                death surrounds you in a
                vortex, as if to whisper,
                Memento Mori my dear.
                everyone and everything flashes—
                bright beams radiate in your heart.
                still, you accept this is the end.

his arms thrust into you,
and you can breathe again.
but you've seen the light,
you're wiser.
take your soul, body, and
scars, it's time to leave
for good.

>it may have taken
>longer, but you're
>even stronger.

a new normal

stay in your apartment, go to class,
fill your prescription, and try to relax.
wake up unable to recognize the girl
in the mirror—try your best not to hurl.

depressions hold is strong and class
is harder to get to…you need a pass.
disability services receive your letter,
they plan to help you till you're better.

you become stale with every move,
just go through the motions in a groove.
erase your existence and don't be alive,
push yourself off the earth to survive.

no communication

you know nothing, you're in the dark.
in your mind you try to let go, but
curiosity is hard to catch and kill.
you wonder, but you won't know.

there is no talking, you and them.
wait. wait. wait. wait. wait.
for the news to come, and rest—
you'll need that energy to fight.

therapy the flashbacks away

sleep in bed, the same place that almost killed you.
try to get comfortable, try to forget, and don't ever
look up. see your therapist, she can help you through.
hope to find a way to cope, or sleep like this forever.

rest deep and serene, until you cannot breathe anymore—
you're choking on air and gasping, but it was only a dream.
this reoccurring nightmare isn't something you can ignore.
reliving this haunting death is becoming more extreme.

take the tools she gives you and use them routinely—
these are your only weapons now. just get through a night.
meditate, wear the 15 lb. blanket, and sleep serenely—
don't forget your pill. only then will you sleep tonight.

many nights on martin st.

lime flavored carbonated water pours over room temperature silver tequila in clear plastic cups with ornate bubble-like designs & sits on the coffee table near the window's edge where pane meets pain & overlooks people walking on cracked pavement & inside you sit lathered in tanning solution on the light blue couch cover hovering over the white loveseat & hold a pillow in your lap inhaling & exhaling between notes of loomy lamb playlist tunes & somewhere you find an empowering sense of peace, of self-love.

insects crawl to the surface

creepy crawly insect legs run fast—
inch by inch by inch they crawl.
slowly pushing through skin and
bloodshot facial scars with fury.

not even a thousand needles piercing
could hurt so bad—*or could they?*
unable to move in excruciating pain,
they ask; *are you having a stroke?*

if only they knew the foul sensations,
the eerie tingles of electricity imploding.
nerves work hard beneath your skin—
crossed fingers hope the flame reignites.

learning to drive your face

no, you weren't born with it,
but it's your reality now.

no matter how many ants march on your face,
nerves won't rekindle—
death can't always be revived.
learn to control them without feeling,
go back to driving school.
let water, food, saliva fall out.

you'll get it one day,
they won't even notice.

silicone slumbers

bloodshot facial scars draw attention—
this is the show they gawk around for.
avoid the sun and accept a new friend,
thick gelled silicone is by your bedside.

silicone deeply hydrating the scar, and
reducing harsh collagen fiber production.
apply each night before bed and sleep,
now repeat it and don't miss a beat.

in your slumber it reduces the redness,
reduces the stare appeal. it flattens, it
softens, it even pales, you must apply
daily and follow doctor's strict orders.

so, sleep, sleep away in your lonely
silicone slumber—aided with one
sweet sleeping pill, just to keep
the flashbacks away for a night.

be prepared

communication starts, you are told
only what you absolutely must know.
the rest, well, the rest is best left off
your tongue—there are things to deny.

go through the motions and practice,
practice the scene. you will be all
alone tomorrow, just you and the
lawyer in a room full of vicious foes.

they will ask you this, and that,
how will you carefully respond?

remember you will be under oath,
it's okay if you say *i don't know.*
don't give them too much insight,
just enough—a robot in adolescence.

oh, and no matter what they do or
say, you'll need to shake their hands
and say, *thank you for your time.*
after all, we don't want you labeled…

DIFFICULT

tomorrow will be a long and hard fight,
so, get some rest—please try your best.
be prepared for the fight of a lifetime,
be prepared for injustice served hot.

good cop, bad cop

good cop, bad cop, an American tale as old as time.
but this time you're not just playing good cop, bad cop,
this time you're all alone tango dancing with the devil—
naked and afraid, get ready to gamble with your soul.

lay your left hand on the cold brown leather bible,
there's no turning back now—spotlight on you.
*i solemnly swear and declare that i will tell the truth,
the whole truth, and nothing but the truth.*

good cop goes first, she wants to make you feel comfy—
give you a false sense of, don't worry *you're in good hands.*
her questions hit the surface level, asking to learn more,
more about what actually happened to you that night.

the two of you dance back and forth for over an hour,
but you only share what she asks for between each
black cherry cough drop…nothing more than she asks.
the good cop is done, which means you get a break.

go to the bathroom, take a breath, look in the mirror,
you're halfway there. you tell your lawyer this has been
easy so far—the reaction looks grave, the worst must be
yet to come, so stay focused…you mustn't let them bury you.

it's bad cops turn and he turns to you with wicked eyes—
he *knows a thing or two because he's seen a thing or two.*
his questions will not be hitting the surface level, but
rather formulated to expose you raw—let part two begin.

this tango is far more deadly than the first one, he turns
pulling out a tall stack of white paper with yellow highlights.
boom. boom. boom. boom. boom. he fires away with force,
asking you what you meant or said in therapy date by date.

oh, how your eyes ask him for mercy, he won't come to your
aid—what he wants is the worst you, served up on a plate.

he speaks with force, moves aggressively, and looks down,
down at you like you are nothing but an ant under his shoe.
those sessions, those notes were meant to be confidential,
but the system favors the corporation not the injured victim.

terrified of what he'll do next, you try not to show it—conceal.
he chuckles to himself, as if you are stupid, and bluntly asks,
were you sexual assaulted or what? tell me what happened?
oh, he wants to make you cry, cry right now and he'd be happy.

sorrow boils within you, but you stir in down—internalizing.
speechless struggling to find a response you look over,
internally shouting for help, *help me and pull me out.*
your lawyer can't block it—submit to the dehumanizing words.

shakily you explain how the situation he's referring to was an
emotionally and physically abusive relationship from years ago.
but he wants more, he came for blood and won't leave without—
a token of his stellar performance for his end of year review.

pushing and pushing he forces you to share how your abuser
hit, punched, and choked you—he wants you to crumble,
but you won't give him the satisfaction. swallow the tears
and take a breath, you don't want to be labeled **EMOTIONAL**.

have you been injured since the ceiling collapsed on you?

he sets the trap with a simple question, an interpretable question—
a dramatic dip in your deadly dance. he can't wait to bury you, to
ruin your character—he'd give anything to paint you a big fat liar.
but you're already two moves ahead of him—he's just unaware.

i don't know. i mean when you frame it like that someone could interpret "being injured" as falling off of a bike and scrapping a knee and someone else could interpret it as going to the hospital. So, when you frame it like that, i just don't know.

you've let him have a taste of that internal boiling sensation,
and he doesn't like it—he stammers to find his next words.
the rest of the dance following a similar tempo—it's almost been
3 full hours of interrogation. still, you tango on with the devil.

closing remarks are made—your body more tense than ever—
and just before the stenographer can stop keeping record, you…
thank you for your time today. as the words leave your mouth,
your stomach turns sick. at least it's over, you did it—for now.

there will be no pancakes today

growing up you always loved
warm Mickey Mouse pancakes—
with whipped cream, sprinkles,
chocolate chips, and a cherry.

mom and dad feel helpless,
knowing you were all alone
in there. they offer to take
you out for some pancakes.

you don't know what you
need, so you easily agree.
hop in the car, along for
the ride—trying to hide.

silently you cry and cry,
watering invisible flowers
with each drop, drop, drop.
your emotions drench you.

no one can hear you, no,
but mom can see you crying.
let's not get pancakes today,
how about we just go home.

rally and finish this

i can't do this.

uh uh uh uh…

i can't do this.

ahhhhh wahhh…

i can't do this.

alone in your car you break down,
you cry everything out of you and
drain your body of its brutal toxicity.
still muscles tense, no relief in sight.

dark thoughts linger in your mind—
bury them. don't let them break you.
you're stronger, braver, more resilient
than that. figure it out and finish this.

muscles don't relax when tension is home

tightly wound wires don't move,
tense binds hold them in spiraled
knots. your back muscles prove
this to be true as they are stifled.

too tense, for too long, they weep
every time you move. hold your
posture, don't even make a peep.
accept that *the body keeps the score.*

for days, weeks, months, the tension
crept beneath your shiny metal coat.
if only there was a way for prevention,
you wouldn't have to drown in this moat.

take the pain, and carry the weight with class.
at least you're not walking on broken glass.

thanks, Country Bears©

oh, thanks, Country Bears©—for the joy.
take my mind away from reality,
and make me laugh and sing songs to enjoy.
you brighten up my whole mentality.
in class, wishing to be home with the bear crew—
that is the only time you feel happy.
from kickin' it into gear to the heart,
no one can watch them close and feel crappy.
the Country Bears© are what gets you through,
what keeps you going and not turning blue.
it's silly, but let's not grow apart.

oh, thanks, Country Bears©—for the peace.
the whole feature film is comedy gold,
and nothing could make the blunt love decrease.
each bear loves themselves and is so bold—
you wish you had strong confidence like that.
over and over, you watch on repeat—
somehow the story never gets too old.
if only one day we could hug and meet,
whatever the fee was you would pay flat.
maybe we would sing together or chat?
well, you guess that story remains untold.

oh, thanks, Country Bears©—for the embrace.
you couldn't do this without all of them.
to you, they are like a drug—a big dose.
when the harsh words come, they get you through.
they teach all about loving who you are,
and the importance of family love.
you cry when you get their soundtrack CD.
you bring me peace like a graceful white dove,
cascading here and there, but never far.
strum, strum, strum away play that bear guitar.
oh, thanks, Country Bears©—they bandage you speedy.

time passes

every day you make your morning coffee,
take a sip and then dip into the shower.
chilled water makes it easy to stay awake.
don't forget your meds and CBD—essentials.

go to your in-office assistantship, go to class—
you're getting your graduate degree now.
your motions are rhythmic like Lime LaCroix
bubbling in a cup of tequila—just keep going.

---

but sometimes you feel so helpless, so sad.
utterly alone in your one-bedroom apartment,
sipping, swiping, and huffing in the window.
you just want this all to be over, a new leaf.

you grow close with your grad school cohort,
and they offer nice distractions. one of them
becomes a close friend for a snippet of your
lifelong timeline—but friends can be fickle.

COVID-19, a new normal storms the earth.
hide away, stay safe, sanitize, and don't die.
back home your routine is different, but still
you go to your assistantship; you go to class.

inflatable pools, drinking Jenga, and movies—
envy is ugly, be satisfied with what you have.
be patient, everyone is scared and everyone
matters—forget about your case for a moment.

---

swipe, swipe, swipe, and match away,
and let yourself mindlessly be free.
you see him, he sees you, very slowly
things happen—he's your new medicine.

you're now together, inseparable—
the broken and her 6'4" boney crutch.
but he likes that you're broken, in fact,
that's what he likes most, yes a lot.

but wait, there's more

your family always loved museums—
especially your younger sister. for her,
they brought joy. the weather was
nice and so a family outing felt right.

it was a nice family day, all together
engaging with history and taking
selfies along the relaxing canal.
briefly things seemed normal.

the next morning comes around
and you've got to get your things
to go back to school—but wait,
there's more, you can't leave now.

the defense has decided to pull
out one more stop, one more trick.
wouldn't they love to postpone
your deposition…drag things out.

in order for your case to stick,
you now have to go to a doctor—
of their choosing—for a formal
psychological examination.

but wait, there's even more,
they want to record all of this
on candid camera—for what,
who knows, but they want it.

no. no. no. no. no.

you don't want to, but you
have to. clear your schedule,
set the date, and please no
recording—a compromise.

snakes are alive and well

remember they're watching,
this whole thing is a test. so,
you'd better look and act your
best. just smile and keep walking.

you wait for the elevator, and
walk in alone—a stranger follows.
smile kindly from behind painted lips,
and let inquisitive questions flow.

you're short, but sweet and to
the point. finally, the 3rd floor.
get off, find the office, and get
in line to check-in, you got this.

hissssss. hissssss. hissssss. hissssss.

welcome to the snake den,
they're alive, well, and
waiting for you to arrive.
now, wait so they can watch.

the doctor slithers from the door,
greets you, and guides your back
with his hand to a conference room.
now sit, he says with a dirty smile.

the ceiling a main topic at first,
a good ole' cross examination of
answers. the doctor's face twisting
and turning as you share trauma.

shit, he makes you feel like shit.
even when you say *i don't know,*
he pushes and pushes and digs—
a T. Rex playing with its prey.

like the others he questions
your PTSD, unable to grasp
that it's possible to have two
separate forms of trauma.

did your abuser ever knock you out?

not under oath, but with honesty,
you say, *i don't know.* but that's
not good enough, so he chips
away at you with sharp words.

maybe you've been hit on the head so many times your memory is bad.

are you even a reliable source for your trauma?

internalize, conceal, don't let
it phase you…let it hit your
metal surface and politely
disagree. don't be **RUDE**.

now, he moves to your breast,
exposing non-elective surgeries.
a master at exploitation, he's
focused on your lifetime of scars.

*why aren't you insecure about your chest scars on a daily basis,
like your facial scar?*

really, this is really happening,
he is really acting like you walk
around with your whole chest
exposed everyday—is he insane.

release some tension, it's almost
over—but wait honey there's more.
a manual 567 true or false question
personality test awaits your answers.

alone now, taking the test, you know
they're watching you and every move.
none of the questions go together—
are they trying to prove insanity?

finish the test and leave—don't let him
walk you to the car. stop him and slither
away slowly. be friendly and smile. dad
awaits you, don't make a scene—get out.

can we settle this?

mediate, mediate, mediate, just try to find a compromise.
a jury trial isn't really necessary—*is it?* just imagine all those
eyes on you, all eyes on you, yes, they're glued to you.

they'll offer something low because to them, you're
just a number. not an injured person who faced death
and an unrelenting cycle of pre-post-traumatic stress.

don't let them sell you short, you know your worth
and you're worth more than that—what if you kept
your original face, *would you have taken it for granted?*

their only argument—paid for from their corrupt doctor—
is that you're **FRAGILE.** it's laughable,
how could someone so **FRAGILE** *be resilient through
what you went through?*

one, two, three, four, five, six, seven, eight, nine, ten.
ten days back and forth, still they relentlessly fight you.
but in the end they're too afraid to go against you.

can we settle this? yes, we can!

Part III

26 months later...

26 months later, you walk the steps of
the historic military house—preserved—
in a little neighborhood of other fort homes.
take a seat in the conference room and sign.

it's really over, there will be no more
bloodshed. all you have to do now is
try, try, try, try to move on—be bold.
break out of that robot shell and live.

you've been in hiding for so long, be you
now—*do you know who you are anymore?*
of course not, why would you. month by
month, they took that away from you.

try, try, try, try to find yourself again—
she's hiding down there somewhere.
they tell you you're irritable, they tell
you you're this and that—*is it true?*

26 months later, it's time to leave the steps of
the historic military house behind you. emerge,
emerge with strength and sing your victory song.
get out of the muddy waters, and rediscover you.

reflective awakening

crazy dreams filled your mind last night,
write them down to draw the connecting lines.

look into the mirror

your eyes are growing nearer,
but who is in the mirror?

no, you didn't recognize,

        but then it got clearer,

                awaken and see through the mirror no it doesn't have to be so bad

        open that passage to the past, do it,

      don't miss the point,

just listen to the voices and cross the glass brick road,

      dance through the mirror,

cry through the mirror,

      walk through the mirror a new vessel.

you are the wolf

within every woman there lives a wolf,
a powerful force of knowledge and life.
fierce, smart, and strong is the lone wolf,
but with her pack, she cuts like a knife.

they were wrong about your fragile mind.
a wild woman of magic, holistic medicine,
and instinct—don't you leave her behind.
she is part of you, so trust her medicine.

connect with your inner spirit and find
what you've been missing—that taste,
touch, smell, sound, you've yet to find.
strength is a gift; it must be embraced.

you are the wolf, the strong resilient
woman—now, go run with your pack.

EMDR

1…2….3

sink, sink deep into the colored shapes
bouncing around on your black screen.
listen to the classical notes and the
pure full tones they throw into space.

let your mind guide you, let it explore
the deepest of your psyche—learn more.
remember the pain, the sorrow, the fear
of accepting death or thanking your abuser.

see the scenes in the mirror, taste the
black cherry drop, hear the cries, touch
the face's scar, it's time to relive it all.
water flowers and get it out, purge it.

go deeper. go further back in time.
remember your constant fear, the
power he held over you at age 16.
no dignity, no self-worth, no love.

relive the punches and feel hands
pressing on your throat, a swift
whip of the belt and a chuckle,
no one will ever love you, only me.

reorganize the library and fill in the
missing blanks. know what happened,
own your life's story—hold onto it tight.
give yourself care, give yourself grace.

3-months later, the finish line in sight.
you've done it, you've done the hard
work—most others would've run away.
thanks, thanks everyone for patience.

the brain waters the aloe plant

you and your brain went through hell.
everything stacked for them, against you,
but you didn't need the cheat sheet. See,
you knew you'd be strong; keep going.

now, your brain waters the luscious
aloe plant that is your body. she heals
herself holistically from within. never
dwelling on what could have been.

brain neurons drip. drip. drip. drip.
and the aloe plant drinks and grows,
she grows even stronger than before.
you're flourishing the middle finger.

still, you wonder how they sleep at night.
you hope, no you pray they'll change—
it's not likely though. you hope maybe,
just maybe one day the cycle can end.

you've outgrown him

he liked that you were broken, in fact,
that's what he liked most, yes a lot.
it drew him close, made him feel
oh, so needed—he liked you weak.

with you growing stronger each day,
he felt himself being thrown to the
side. you no longer holding onto him
tight for support—no more crutches.

going behind your back, making future plans—
he wears you like an accessory.
when you learn the long-lived lies,
you cry, but realize you've outgrown him.

you don't need his love.
no, you don't want to be loved.
you don't need to make up.
no, you don't want to make up.

you once cared for him, but you've outgrown
him. it's time to move on, grab your baggage,
and go. there should be no pressure from
the ones who love you, he doesn't love you.

embrace you

> *"We aren't born hating our bodies,
> it's something the world teaches us."*
> Taryn Brumfitt

remember when you were a little girl,
a much simpler time. it didn't matter
what you wore or the size of pores,
you were just happy to live life full.

you used to love the special treatment,
in your blonde wig and unhealthy skin.
but now, you hate the stares of attention.
where did that little girl's happiness go?

your face may sit different, it may look
different too, but that woman is still you.
change the direction and seek out your joy,
no one is going to deliver it in a glass bottle.

true beauty is kindness, humility, self-love,
compassion, empathy, and care—this beauty
lies within you. so, embrace yourself, scar and
all. embrace and shine your light—live life full.

you are…

you are resilient, strong, and unbreakable—
a perseverant fighter who is NOT fragile.

you are fearful, yet brave and courageous—
ready for anything that comes your way.

you are the fierce wolf who runs with her pack—
an empowered female leader and mentor.

you are alive, a lilac flower in spring blooming from the breath of life—
still memento mori.

you are flesh, and bones reconstructed from decay—
literally.

you are energy bubbling through the weight on top of you—
light and life through the debris.

you are intelligent, educated, and intuitive—
book and life smart.

you are analytical and cautious with self and spatial awareness—
present in the moment.

you are eccentric, unique, and special—
a precious peanut in a world of cashews.

you are hard loving, compassionate, and empathetic—
putting others whom you love first.

you are loyal, protective, and supportive—
doing whatever it takes.

you are gentle, helpful, thoughtful, and generous—
willing to give more than you receive.

you are observant, quiet, and mysterious—
but vocal and transparent when you need to be.

you are friendly, warm, cold, and distant all at once—
it depends on the relationship.

you are multi-talented and ambitious, but still humble—
a lifelong learner at heart.

you are bold, real, and authentic—
yourself no matter what others think, yet still self-conscious.

you are likeable, reliable, and trustworthy—
a level of comfort and trust lies with you.

you are the one who tells my brain to water the aloe plant that is my body—
we are connected.

you are thankful, tranquil, and at peace—
no day is given, and life is too short to hold anger

you are a paintbrush on life's canvas, swirling in a sea of unknowns—
the final painting unclear.

let him in and see the flowers bloom

work on yourself, care and love yourself—
do that and you don't need anyone else.
inviting someone in can only lead to hurt.
you love yourself, so you don't need love.

no, being in love only leaves you vulnerable—
ready to be hurt, abandoned, and lonely again.
the mindset doesn't waiver here, you're still
holding strong—by all means protect yourself.

chat on dating apps for fun—don't get too close.
screen through facetime, go out, block, repeat.
a well-oiled machine of running and hiding.
see him like your profile and accept.

he's younger, but he's sweet and values align.
go on dates, watch the Country Bears©, talk for
hours, and settle in for a while. the lens is
shifting, *can you help but change with it too?*

he wants you to learn that flowers will return—
you deserve love and do want to be loved.
it will take you time and he's patient enough,
just be open and flowers will return in bloom.

memento mori

death
/deTH/

noun
the action or fact of dying or being killed; the end of the life of a person or organism.

memento mori—remember you must die.
the phrase no longer so terrifying or gray.
you hold it close; you wear it on your arm,
and remember how precious loved ones are.

in life you can reflect, but there's no looking back.
things keep going, things keep moving—you do too.
whatever happened to you in the past is history,
and tomorrow is waiting, blooming with possibility.

time goes by fast, sometimes too fast, which
is why it's important to slow down and take
each moment in. you never know how long
you have, but that's the beauty—the unknown.

embrace yourself and embrace the unknown,
it's okay to let go of control—someone's got you.
forever more, memento mori will beat inside you
with each lup-dup, lup-dup, lup-dup, lup-dup…

don't let the shackles of the past bind you tightly.
be curious, be open, and stay the resilient wolf.
clear the muddy waters and start your life over,
you'll earn you're much stronger than before.

memento mori,

        there's no looking back

                take those scars and don't look back.

Eileen Porzuczek is a creative writer, artist, and professional storyteller. She has a B.A. in English—with concentrations in creative writing and professional writing—and an M.A. in Emerging Media Design and Development—with concentrations in design thinking, transmedia storytelling, user experience, and user interaction—from Ball State University.

Eileen has worked with Ball State University and the Indiana Writers Center to bring community memoirs to life through creative writing. Some of the memoir anthologies she's worked on include: *#KeepMuncieWeird…AndWhimsical!*, *Grit, Grace, and Gratitude: Senior Citizen Sage Stories*, and multiple editions of *I Remember: Indianapolis Youth Write About Their Lives*.

Eileen has won poetry awards like Apoetical's Poet's Choice Award, and her poems have been published in *Creation Magazine*, *New Plains Review*, *Sheepshead Review*, and more. *Memento Mori: A Poetic Memoir in Three Parts*, published by Finishing Line Press, is Eileen's debut poetry collection. She has been working on putting this poetic memoir together in the years following her accident and is thankful to have a platform to share her story.

Eileen currently lives in the Greater Indianapolis area with her partner and their rescue Goldendoodle. In her free time, she enjoys reading, painting, playing cards, and spending time with friends and family.

www.ingramcontent.com/pod-product-compliance
Lightning Source LLC
Chambersburg PA
CBHW030057170426
43197CB00010B/1560